YOUNG SCIENTIST CONCEPTS & PROJECTS

MACHINES

CHRIS OXLADE

Gareth Stevens Publishing
MILWAUKEE

The original publishers would like to thank the following children, and their parents, for modeling in this book: Nana Addae, Maria Bloodworth, Ricky Edward Garrett, Sasha Haworth, Alex Lindblom-Smith, Sophie Lindblom-Smith, Laura Masters, Jessica Moxley, Aidan Mulcahy, Fiona Mulcahy, Seán Mulcahy, Jamie Rosso, and Joe Westbrook.

Gareth Stevens Publishing would like to thank Kenneth Mischka for his assistance with the accuracy of the text. Mr. Mischka is Chair of the Aviation Maintenance Technician program at Milwaukee Area Technical College, Milwaukee, Wisconsin, where he also teaches courses in physics and electronics.

For a free color catalog describing Gareth Stevens' list of high-quality books and multimedia programs, call 1-800-542-2595 (USA) or 1-800-461-9120 (Canada). Gareth Stevens Publishing's Fax: (414) 225-0377. See our catalog, too, on the World Wide Web: http://gsinc.com

Library of Congress Cataloging-in-Publication Data

Oxlade, Chris.
Machines / by Chris Oxlade.
p. cm. — (Young scientist concepts and projects)
Includes bibliographical references and index.
Summary: Describes various types of machines, how they are used, and how they work. Includes fact boxes and suggested activities and projects.
ISBN 0-8368-2163-7 (lib. bdg.)
1. Machinery—Juvenile literature. [1. Machinery. 2. Machinery— Experiments. 3. Experiments.] I. Title. II. Series.
TJ147.O85   1998
621.8—dc21   98-19938

This North American Edition first published in 1998 by
Gareth Stevens Publishing
1555 North RiverCenter Drive, Suite 201
Milwaukee, WI 53212 USA

Original edition © 1998 by Anness Publishing Limited.
First published in 1998 by Lorenz Books, an imprint of Anness Publishing Inc., New York, New York.
This U.S. edition © 1998 by Gareth Stevens, Inc.
Additional end matter © 1998 by Gareth Stevens, Inc.

Editor: Charlotte Evans
Consultant: Graham Peacock
Photographer: John Freeman
Stylist: Melanie Williams
Designer: Caroline Grimshaw
Picture researcher: Marion Elliot
Illustrator: Nick Hawken
Gareth Stevens series editor: Dorothy L. Gibbs
Editorial assistant: Diane Laska

Printed in the United States of America

1 2 3 4 5 6 7 8 9 02 01 00 99 98

MACHINES

CONTENTS

WHAT IS A MACHINE?

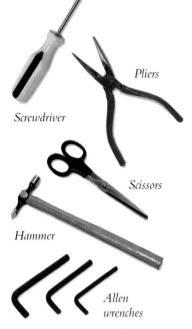

Screwdriver

Pliers

Scissors

Hammer

Allen wrenches

All these tools are simple machines found in most homes. They all do jobs that would be much more difficult to do without them.

T HOUSANDS of different devices are machines, from calculators to trucks, although many of them do not look like something you would think of as a machine. Scissors and staplers are very simple machines; computers and cars are very complicated ones. All machines, however, have one thing in common — they help us do jobs, which makes our lives easier. Think about what you did yesterday and write down every machine you used or saw, from the time you woke up to the time you went to sleep. Wherever we are and whatever we are doing, we are surrounded by machines. Their help is vital to us. Many things we take for granted, such as opening a tin can or tightening a screw, can be done only with a machine.

The screws used to make this model helicopter are machines. They work by holding the model's parts together.

Using tools

This girl is using a wrench to tighten the nuts on a model helicopter. A wrench is a simple tool used to tighten or loosen nuts and bolts. By using the wrench instead of her fingers, she can fasten the nuts tighter, making them more secure.

FACT BOX

• Leonardo da Vinci (1452–1519), an Italian artist and inventor, drew plans for machines, such as tanks and aircraft, that were centuries ahead of their time.

• Greek scientist Hero of Alexandria invented a steam engine, a slot machine, and a screw press in the first century A.D.

Old machines

This fifteenth-century painting shows people using many different machines to help them farm the land. Some of the first machines ever invented were used by farmers. At the bottom of the painting is a plow; on the right-hand side is a waterwheel. At the very top is a machine called a shaduf, which was used to bring up water from a well.

Huge machines, such as cranes, can be found on construction sites. These machines have powerful engines for moving and lifting soil, rocks, steel, and concrete.

This woman is using an ax to chop large logs into smaller pieces. When she brings the ax down, the sharp blade slices into the wood, forcing it to split apart. The ax is a simple machine, but it is very effective.

A computer does not help us lift, move, or cut things, but it makes life easier by remembering information and doing calculations. Computers help us work much faster and more accurately.

THE FIRST MACHINES

ALL machinery is based on the elements found in six simple machines: the lever; the wheel and axle; the inclined plane, or ramp; the wedge; the screw; and the pulley. All six of these machines have been used for thousands of years, but the simplest, and probably the oldest, is the lever. Any rod or stick can act as a lever to help move heavy objects or pry things apart. A lever is a bar or a rod that tilts on a pivot. A small effort pushing down on the longer end of the bar can raise a large weight on the shorter end nearer the pivot. Using a lever makes the power of your push much greater, which is called a mechanical advantage. There are several different types of levers. Some have just one lever arm; others have two lever arms joined together by a pivot.

A door is a simple lever that pivots on hinges. Closing a door at the handle is much easier than pressing near the hinge.

Using a simple lever

This girl is using a spoon as a lever to lift the lid off a can of paint. The lever arm pivots on the rim of the can. As the girl pushes down on the long end, the shorter end, wedged under the lid, pushes up with great force, making the stiff lid move.

Force

Pivot

Load

How a lever works

A force, such as a push or a pull, is put on one part of the lever arm to overcome the weight or resistance of an object, which is called the load.

Levers and lifting

This boy is using a ruler as a lever to lift a book. When the pivot, a small box, is placed close to the book, the pushing force needed to lift the book is less than the weight of the book.

When the pivot is moved to the middle of the lever, the force needed to lift the book is equal to the weight of the book. The force and the load are the same.

When the pivot is moved closer to where the boy is pushing, more force is needed to lift the book. The pushing force must now be greater than the weight of the book.

This lever machine (above), called a shaduf, is being used to water fields. A long pole with a bucket on one end pivots on a frame. A pulling force on another long pole, attached to the lever arm, brings up water in the bucket.

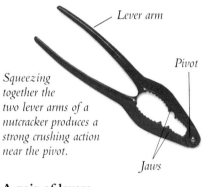

Lever arm

Pivot

Squeezing together the two lever arms of a nutcracker produces a strong crushing action near the pivot.

Jaws

A pair of levers
Like scissors or pliers, a nutcracker has two lever arms joined at a pivot. Squeezing the ends of the nutcracker arms together crushes a nut placed between its jaws. The levers make the squeezing force about four times stronger, breaking the nut quite easily.

LEVERS AND BALANCE

Levers are not used just for lifting, cutting, and crushing. A lever on a central pivot can be made to balance. The lever will balance if the amount of force on one side of the pivot is the same as the amount of force on the other side. A playground teeter-totter, or seesaw, is a balancing lever. It is a plank balanced on a center post, or pivot. Someone small and light can balance a much bigger person by sitting on it in the right position. Balancing levers have important uses, comparing the size of one force to the size of another force. For example, a weighing machine, called a balance scale, measures the weight of an object by comparing it with standard weights, such as ounces (grams) and pounds (kilograms).

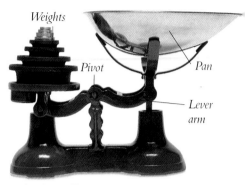

This kind of balance scale was once used for weighing things in stores and in the kitchen. To make the lever arm balance, the weights on the left must equal the weight in the pan.

Using a balance scale
To weigh something with a balance scale, put it into the pan on one end of the lever arm. Add weights to the other end of the arm until the arm balances. The total amount of individual weights added will be the weight of whatever is in the pan.

A Roman lever balance
This carving of a Roman scale is from the first century A.D. The object to be weighed was put inside the sack, and a large weight was moved backward and forward until the arm balanced.

Two boys of equal weight can make the lever arm of a seesaw balance by sitting the same distance away from the pivot.

Lever arm   Pivot

Balancing a seesaw

A seesaw *(left)* can show the effect of moving weight closer to or farther away from the pivot of a lever arm.

Adding a friend to one side of the lever arm makes that side heavier. The pushing force of the pair's greater weight easily lifts the lighter weight of the single boy.

FACT BOX

• A trebuchet was used in medieval times to hurl boulders at the enemy up to $1/4$ mile (0.4 kilometers) away. It was a war machine based on the lever arm.

• The ancient Egyptians invented balance scales to weigh gold. Gold was a precious commodity. It had to be weighed accurately.

Moving the heavier weight closer to the pivot, and the lighter weight farther away, will balance the lever arm of the seesaw again.

Investigating balance

Balance a ruler on a tube. Try putting different-sized piles of coins at different positions on each end. One coin will balance two coins if the single coin is twice as far from the pivot.

LEVERS EVERYWHERE

LEVERS are very common machines. These two pages show some of the machines that use levers to work. Each machine has a diagram that identifies the force, pivot, and load to illustrate how the lever works. Lever machines are divided into three different classes, or basic types. The most common type is a first-class lever, where the pivot is always between the load and the force. Balance scales and pliers are types of first-class levers. In a second-class lever, the load is between the pivot and the force. Nutcrackers and wheelbarrows are two examples of second-class levers. In a third-class lever, the force is between the pivot and the load. Hammers and tweezers are third-class levers.

Every key on a piano keyboard is a lever, and each one has other levers attached to it. These levers make a hammer fly quickly against a string when the key is pressed.

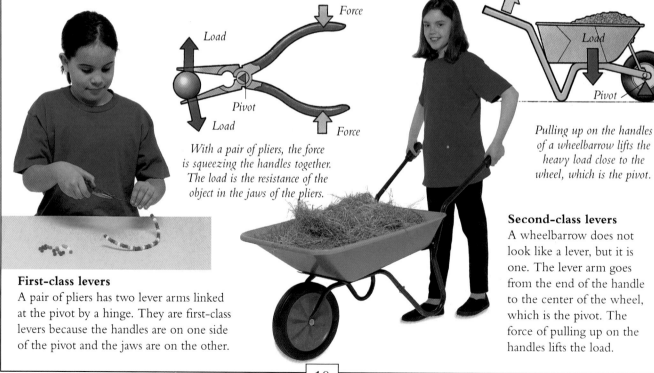

With a pair of pliers, the force is squeezing the handles together. The load is the resistance of the object in the jaws of the pliers.

Pulling up on the handles of a wheelbarrow lifts the heavy load close to the wheel, which is the pivot.

First-class levers
A pair of pliers has two lever arms linked at the pivot by a hinge. They are first-class levers because the handles are on one side of the pivot and the jaws are on the other.

Second-class levers
A wheelbarrow does not look like a lever, but it is one. The lever arm goes from the end of the handle to the center of the wheel, which is the pivot. The force of pulling up on the handles lifts the load.

A hammer is a lever when you use your wrist as a pivot. Your fingers gripping the handle provide the force that moves the hammer's head.

Pivot Force

Load

Third-class levers

A hammer is a lever, even though it doesn't look like one. The handle and your hand together form the lever arm. Your wrist is the pivot. Your fingers supply the force that moves the hammer head down.

A fishing rod is a third-class lever. Lifting a fish out of the water requires a pull much stronger than the weight of the fish. When casting, a small movement of the fisherman's arm flicks the line at the end of the rod a long way.

Your arm is a third-class lever. As it lifts an object, the force is between the pivot and the load.

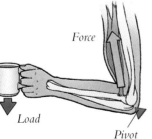

Force

Load

Pivot

Body levers

The bones in your lower arm form a third-class lever, with your elbow as a pivot. A muscle, called the biceps, at the front of your upper arm, provides the effort to lift the weight, or load, in your hand.

MAKING LEVERS WORK

You will need: short pencil, two 6-inch (15-centimeter) strips of wood, 2 thick rubber bands, small objects to pick up or squeeze (such as candy or grapes).

THE projects on these two pages show you how to make two different lever machines. The first machine is a simple gripper for picking up or squeezing objects. Depending on where the force and the load are, it can be a second-class lever, like a nutcracker, or a third-class lever, like a pair of tweezers. In a nutcracker, the load is between the pivot and the force. In a pair of tweezers, the force is between the pivot and the load. Draw a lever diagram for each way to use the gripper to help you understand how second- and third-class levers work. The second machine is a balance scale, like the ones used by the Romans about two thousand years ago. The scale works by balancing the weight of an object with a known weight — in this case, a bag of coins. The coins are moved along the lever arm until they balance the object being weighed. The object's weight is then read off against a scale.

Make a gripper

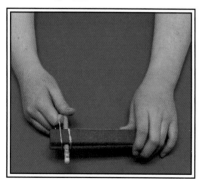

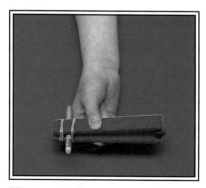

3 Hold the gripper at the other end to make it act like a nutcracker.

1 Put the pencil between the strips of wood, near one end. Wrap the rubber bands tightly around the wood *(as shown)* to make a pivot. The gripper is ready to use.

2 To make the gripper act like a pair of tweezers, hold it near the pivot and squeeze. Try to pick up a soft object, such as a piece of candy or a grape, without squashing it.

MATERIALS

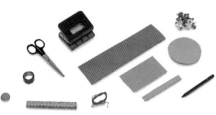

You will need: thick cardboard about 20 x 3 inches (50 x 7.5 cm), thin cardboard, scissors, string, ruler, hole punch, 5-inch (12.5-cm) circle of cardboard, tape, 4 ounces (114 grams) of coins, felt-tip pen, small objects to weigh.

Make a balance scale

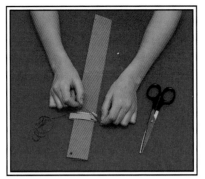

1 Make a lever arm by folding the thick cardboard in half. Attach a loop of thin cardboard to the arm, 4½ inches (11.2 cm) from one end. Tie a piece of string to this loop.

2 Punch a hole ½ inch (1.2 cm) in from the same end of the arm. Shape the cardboard circle into a cone and tie it to the hole. Make an envelope and attach a loop of string.

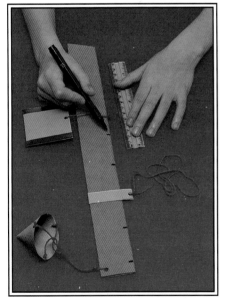

3 Hang the envelope over the arm and seal the coins in it. Starting at the center of the cardboard loop, make a mark every 2 inches (5 cm) along the arm. Use this scale to weigh the objects.

4 Put an object in the cone and slide the envelope of coins backward and forward along the arm until the arm balances. Each mark along the scale equals 1½ ounces (42 g). So the object in this picture *(right)* weighs about 2½ ounces (71 g).

WHEELS AND AXLES

The pedals on a tricycle are a wheel and axle. Pushing on the pedals turns the axle and drives the tricycle's front wheel.

T HE wheel is one of the most important inventions ever made. About six thousand years ago, people discovered that using logs as rollers was a more efficient way to move heavy loads. A slice from a log was the first wheel, and a pole connected to a wheel was an axle. Turning the wheel makes the axle turn, too. Although a wheel on the end of an axle might not seem like a machine, it is, because turning the axle using the wheel is easier than turning the axle itself. Wheels and axles increase mechanical advantage — turning the wheel makes the axle turn with greater force. The bigger the wheel compared to the size of the axle, the greater the force, which makes turning even easier. Wheels are simple machines used in millions of other machines. One of the most obvious uses is in vehicles.

Wheeled vehicles were in use more than four thousand years ago, and they are still the most common form of transportation today. Sometimes wheel-and-axle machines are difficult to recognize. Can you find a wheel and axle in a wrench — or in a door key?

Handle (wheel)

Spindle (axle)

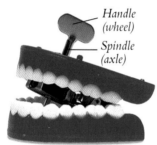

Winding up

The key of a wind-up toy has a handle that is a wheel and a spindle that is an axle. The large handle makes it easier to turn the spindle. Door keys work the same way.

Wheel (wrench handle)

Axle (bolt shaft)

Wrenches and bolts

A wrench and a bolt make up a wheel-and-axle system. The threaded shaft of the bolt is the axle, and the handle of the wrench is the wheel. Turning the wrench makes it much easier to tighten or loosen the bolt.

Cart wheels

This Roman mosaic *(left)*, made about 1,700 years ago, shows a cart full of grapes being pulled by oxen. The wheels and axles on the cart made the oxen able to pull a much heavier load than they could carry on their backs. The first cart wheels were made from slices of tree trunks. Spokes were invented about four thousand years ago.

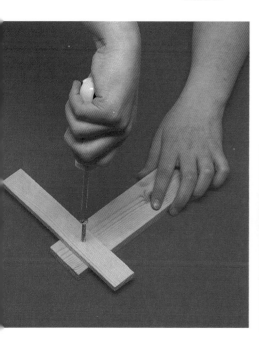

The shaft of a screwdriver is an axle, and the handle is a wheel. The handle increases the twisting force, or torque, on the shaft needed to drive in a screw.

Potters' wheels

One of the first uses of the wheel was to make pots. Simple potters' wheels, such as this one *(above)* in India, are still used around the world. This massive wooden wheel is turned by foot or by hand.

Steering wheels

A car's steering wheel is attached to the end of an axle, called the steering column. The wheel increases the force from the driver's hands, so the driver is able to control the car.

WHEELS AT WORK

THERE are hundreds of different kinds of wheels and axles. Some are very old designs, such as the capstan wheel. A capstan is a wheel on an axle with handles that extend out from the edge of the wheel. The handles are used to turn the wheel, which turns the axle. Large capstan wheels can be turned by animals walking around and around attached to the wheel, or by several people, each pushing on a handle. In the past, capstans were a familiar sight on ships and in dockyards, where they were used to raise heavy loads, such as a ship's anchor. You can make a simple capstan wheel that works in a similar way. At the end of this project, a ratchet is attached to the axle. A ratchet is a very useful device that acts like a catch. It prevents the capstan wheel from turning back on itself after you stop winding it.

This watering machine (above) has a capstan wheel. A person or an animal pushes against a handle on the wheel and walks around and around. The pushing force raises a gate that lets water from a canal flow into the fields.

Make a capstan wheel

1 Draw a pencil guideline about one-third down from the top on two opposite sides of a box. Use a cardboard tube to draw circles on these lines. Cut out the circles.

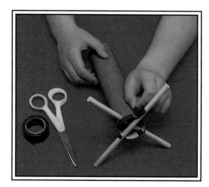

2 Cut four slots in one end of the tube. Lay a dowel into each pair of slots, one dowel crossed over the other. Tape the dowels in place to complete the capstan wheel.

3 Push the tube through the holes in the box. Tape one end of a piece of string to the middle of the tube inside the box. Tie a weight to the other end of the string.

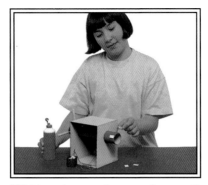

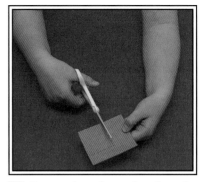

4 Stand the box on the edge of a table so the weight hangs down. Turn the capstan wheel to raise the weight. Try holding the handles at the ends, then closer to the center.

5 To make a ratchet, cut four small cardboard rectangles and glue them to the end of the tube that is opposite the capstan wheel. These rectangles are the ratchet teeth.

6 Cut another piece of cardboard into an *L* shape. Bend one leg of the *L* at a right angle to the other to form the lock that will catch on the ratchet teeth.

MATERIALS

You will need: pencil, small cardboard box, cardboard tube, scissors, 2 thin dowels, tape, string, a weight, thick cardboard, glue.

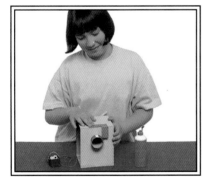

7 Glue the cardboard *L* to the top of the box so the end hanging over the edge will catch in the ratchet teeth. Let the glue dry before testing the ratchet.

8 Turn the capstan wheel to raise the weight again. You should be able to let go of the wheel without the weight dropping. The ratchet teeth will catch on the cardboard lock to stop the axle from turning backward.

INCLINED PLANES

How can an inclined plane, or ramp, be a machine? It makes going uphill, or moving an object uphill against the force of gravity, much easier. Think about people trying to lift a heavy box into a moving van. It might take two people working together to lift the box high enough to put it into the van. One person alone, however, could push the box up a gently sloping ramp. Planks are often used as ramps on a building site. Walking uphill on a winding path is also using a ramp. It is much easier to walk up a gently sloping path that twists and turns than it is to climb straight up a very steep hillside. You have to walk farther along the winding path to reach the top of the hill, but the climb is much easier.

This picture shows the remains of a huge mud-brick ramp used by the ancient Egyptians to build a temple at Karnac about 3,000 years ago.

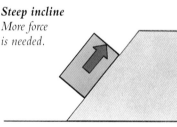

Steep incline
More force is needed.

Gradual incline
Less force is needed.

Steep and gradual
On a steep slope, or incline, all the work is done in a short distance, requiring more force, or effort. On a gradual incline, the work is done over a longer distance, requiring less effort.

Ramps for building
This picture, copied from a painting in an ancient Egyptian tomb, shows a ramp being used to construct a building. Without construction machines, such as cranes, the Egyptians had to build huge sloping ramps to pull stone blocks to the upper levels of a building.

Fast track
When engineers plan roads and highways, they try to avoid having steep inclines. Cuttings and embankments are built into hillsides to make gentle slopes that vehicles can climb without slowing down too much.

Mountain roads

Mountain roads, such as this one in South Africa, zigzag upward in a series of gentle slopes. A road straight up the side of the valley would be far too steep a slope for most vehicles to climb.

FACT BOX

• Some canals have inclined planes, instead of locks, to move boats uphill and downhill. One of these canals in Belgium has an inclined plane 1 mile (1.6 km) long. Boats float inside 5,000-ton (4,537-metric ton) tanks of water that are hauled up the inclined plane on rails.

• The railroad line from Lima to Galera, in Peru, climbs 4 miles (6.4 km). In some places, the track zigzags back and forth across very steep hillsides.

Access ramps

The ramp in this picture goes down to a beach. Ramps make it easier to move on wheels from one level to another. Many public buildings, such as libraries, sports centers, and hospitals, have ramps, as well as stairs, leading to their doors. Without ramps, people in wheelchairs have a very difficult time getting in and out of buildings.

WEDGES AND SCREWS

Wedges and screws are simple machines that work using inclined planes. Think of a wedge as two ramps positioned back-to-back. Although the thin end of a wedge can be pushed into a narrow gap with a small amount of force, the wedge presses with great force against the sides of the gap to spread the gap apart. Chisels, axes, and plows all have wedges; their blades widen from one edge to the other. Screw threads are also a type of inclined plane. They are a long, narrow ramp wrapped around a pole. Screw threads make screws, nuts and bolts, bench vises, and car jacks work. Turning a screw with a small amount of force moves it in or out with greater force.

A wedge can stop a door from opening or closing. Pulling on the door presses the wedge harder against the bottom of the door and the floor.

Wedge cutter

An ax head is a wedge. Its sharp, thin edge sinks into the wood, forcing the wood apart and splitting it. The ax handle makes it possible for a person to swing the ax with great speed and to lever out pieces of wood.

Wedge stripper
Forestry workers use a wedge-shaped tool to strip the bark off tree trunks. The sharp edge of the tool is an inclined plane that cuts and lifts the bark in one movement.

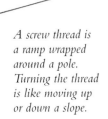

A screw thread is a ramp wrapped around a pole. Turning the thread is like moving up or down a slope.

A spiraling slope

A corkscrew has a thread that winds into a cork as the handle is turned. Turning the handle is quite easy because the thread sinks into the cork only a little with each turn.

Lever arm

Handle

Screw thread inside cork

In this kind of corkscrew, the screw is fully wound into the cork. Then, the lever arms on each side are pushed down to lever out the cork.

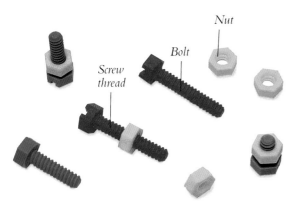

Nut

Bolt

Screw thread

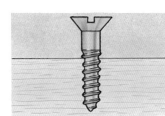

The thread of a wood screw makes it sink into the wood as the screw is turned.

Nuts and bolts

Nuts and bolts make firm joints. The screw thread on a bolt holds a nut and guides it along the bolt when the nut is turned with a wrench. Turning the nut forces it against the head of the bolt, pulling the joint together.

Screws

As a screw turns, its thread bites into the wood. The tip of the screw is wedge-shaped, which helps it push through the wood. Using a screwdriver increases the twisting force, or torque, needed to drive in a screw. Screws are a strong, secure way to hold things together.

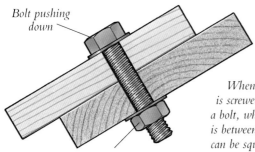

Bolt pushing down

Nut pushing up

When a nut is screwed onto a bolt, whatever is between them can be squeezed tightly together.

PLANES AT WORK

M A T E R I A L S

You will need: long bolt fitted with a nut and a washer, square piece of thin wood or thick cardboard, strong glue, wooden stick, cardboard tube, cardboard, a weight.

RAMPS, wedges, and screws are all adaptations of the inclined plane, which is a lifting device. Although screws are most commonly used to hold things together, they have another important use — the screw jack. A screw jack lifts a huge weight, such as a car, easily, but slowly. The force made by turning the screw thread is used to lift a weight upward instead of creating a tight grip. The project on this page shows how to make a simple type of screw jack. The project on the opposite page shows how to make a device to measure the force needed to lift an object. Try it to see how a more gradual slope makes lifting an object easier.

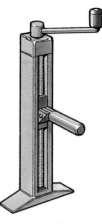

Many cars have a screw jack inside. If a tire goes flat, the driver can lift the car with the jack and change the tire.

Make a screw jack

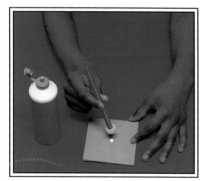

1 Glue the head of a long bolt, with the thread pointing upward, to the middle of a square piece of thin wood or thick cardboard. Let the glue dry.

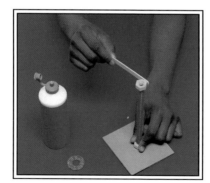

2 Glue the end of a wooden stick to the side of a nut that fits the bolt to make a handle. When the glue is dry, wind the nut onto the bolt and put a washer on top.

3 Glue a cardboard tube to a piece of cardboard. Place the tube over the bolt so it rests on the washer. Turn the handle on the nut to lift a weight.

MATERIALS

You will need: brass paper fastener, rubber band, piece of thick cardboard, string, felt-tip pen, ruler, toy or model vehicle.

Measuring the forces on a slope

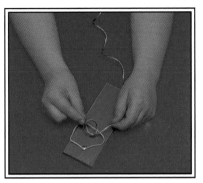

1 Use a paper fastener to attach a rubber band to one end of a 6- x 2-inch (15- x 5-cm) piece of cardboard. Tie a piece of string to the other end of the rubber band.

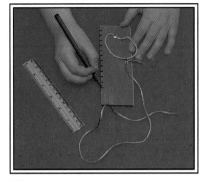

2 Draw a simple scale on the cardboard. Use the scale to record how far the rubber band stretches when it is pulled by a weight. You have made a force measurer.

4 Make a slope by propping up one end of a short plank on some books. How much force is needed to pull the vehicle up this slope? Is it more or less than the vehicle's weight? Lower the slope. Does the force needed to pull the vehicle change? You should find that less force is needed on the lower slope.

3 Attach a toy or model vehicle to the string of the measurer and let it hang. Note where the rubber band stretches to on the scale. Write down this measurement.

PULLEYS

A pulley is a simple machine that is actually a form of the wheel and axle. The simplest pulley system consists of a wheel and a rope. The wheel has a groove in its rim and rotates on an axle. The rope fits into the groove and hangs down on both sides of the wheel. Pulling down on one end of the rope lifts a load attached to the other end. This simple system does not reduce the amount of force needed to lift a load, so there is no mechanical advantage. It does, however, make lifting the load easier, because it is easier to pull down than it is to pull up, or lift. A pulley's special advantage is that it changes the direction of the effort. Using several pulleys together makes lifting even easier. Many pulley systems have more than one pulley wheel. These systems are called block and tackle. Pulleys are useful for lifting loads on building sites and for moving heavy parts and machinery in factories.

A simple pulley changes the direction of the effort needed to lift a load — you pull down instead of up.

Pulleys for building

In this picture from the 1500s, workers are constructing the walls of a great city using a pulley to lift building materials. The worker at the bottom is turning a handle to lift a bucket. The pulley was probably first used in Greece about 2,500 years ago, and it has been in use ever since.

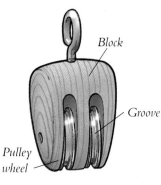

Block

Groove

Pulley wheel

A block and tackle has two blocks (like the one above) arranged one over the other. The pulley wheels are designed to turn easily as the rope in the groove moves around them.

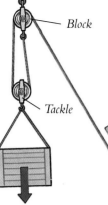

Block

Tackle

Load

Double pulley
This pulley system *(left)* has two pulley wheels. Pulling the rope raises the lower wheel and the load. With two wheels, only half the effort is needed to lift the load, but the rope has to be pulled twice as far.

Effort

This pulley system is a block and tackle. The top pulley wheel, the block, is attached to a set point. The bottom pulley wheel, the tackle, is suspended on a rope passing through the block.

This special pulley system has a high mechanical advantage. A light pull on the loop of chain allows one person to lift a heavy boat engine.

Cranes
Cranes use pulley systems to lift heavy loads. The lifting cables running along this dock crane's arm *(right)* are made of steel.

Pulleys are used to quickly raise and lower lifeboats on a ship. Pulleys are also used on sailboats to raise and lower the sails.

PULLEYS AT WORK

THE projects on these two pages show how pulley systems work. The first project shows how to make a simple double pulley system. This system does not have pulley wheels. Instead, a string passes through smooth metal loops. Metal loops are not as efficient as pulley wheels, but they can show how a pulley system is connected. The second project investigates how adding more turns on a block and tackle reduces the effort needed to move a load. Note, however, that the more turns, the greater the friction. Using wheels in a block and tackle cuts down the friction.

MATERIALS

You will need:
2 large paper clips, pieces of string, a weight.

Heavy-duty block and tackle systems have metal chain links that are much stronger than a rope. The chain links interlock with the shaped pulley wheels.

Make a simple double pulley

1 Tie a large paper clip to a door handle with a short piece of string. Make sure the paper clip is tied securely.

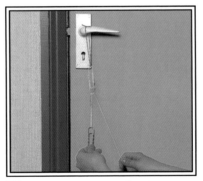

2 Feed a long piece of string through this paper clip's inner loop and through the top loop of another paper clip. Tie one end to the outer loop of the top clip.

3 Use another short piece of string to attach a weight to the bottom paper clip. Pull the end of the long string to lift the bottom paper clip, which will lift the weight.

M A T E R I A L S

You will need:
2 broom handles or thick
dowels, strong string or
thin rope, 2 friends.

Make a block and tackle

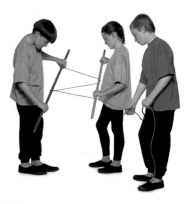

1 Have each of your two friends hold a broom handle or dowel with one hand positioned at each end. Tie the end of a long piece of string or rope to one of the handles.

2 Wrap the string around each handle once, keeping the loops fairly close together on the handles. Then, pull on the string. How easy was it to pull your friends together?

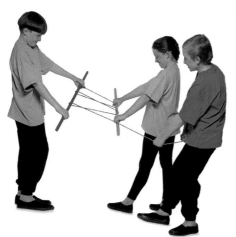

3 Wrap the string twice around each handle. Be sure to keep the turns close together. Pull on the string again. Do you notice anything different this time? Was pulling any easier?

4 Make more turns around the handles and pull again. Do more turns require less pulling effort? Do you have to pull the rope any farther than before?

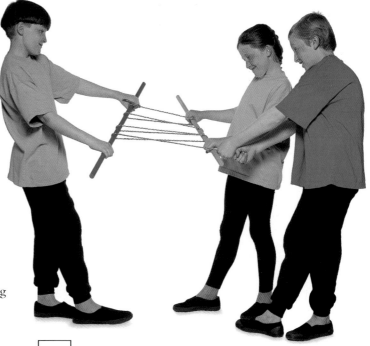

GEARWHEELS

GEARS are wheels with teeth around the edge. They are used to transmit movement from one wheel to another. When two gearwheels are put next to each other, their teeth can interlock so that turning one wheel will make the other wheel turn, too. If both wheels are the same size, they turn at the same speed. If one wheel is bigger than the other, they can be used to speed up or slow down movement, or to increase or decrease a force. Many different machines, from eggbeaters to trucks, have gears to make them work. Belt drives and chain drives are similar to gears, but the two wheels are linked together with a belt or a chain instead of teeth. They, too, transfer power and movement from one shaft to another, and speed can be varied by changing the size of the wheels.

In this simple gear system, one gearwheel turns the other because the teeth interlock. The bigger wheel makes the smaller wheel turn faster because it is twice the size of the smaller one.

Transmitting a force
A set of gears in the center of this eggbeater transmits the turning movement of the handle to the blades of the whisks. The gears speed up the movement, making the blades spin faster than the handle turns.

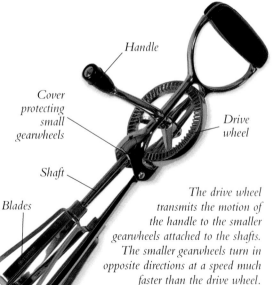

Handle

Cover protecting small gearwheels

Drive wheel

Shaft

Blades

The drive wheel transmits the motion of the handle to the smaller gearwheels attached to the shafts. The smaller gearwheels turn in opposite directions at a speed much faster than the drive wheel.

28

Bicycle gears

Bicycle gears use wheels and a chain to transmit movement from the pedals to the bicycle's rear wheel. As a rider pushes the pedals, the drive wheel turns, moving a chain that turns one of the gearwheels attached to the rear wheel. Moving the chain to a different gearwheel changes the number of times the rear wheel turns each time the pedals go around. The number of turns affects the bike's speed.

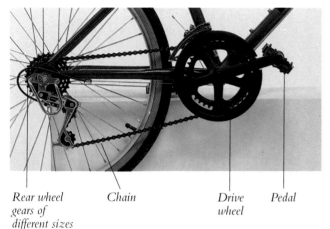

Rear wheel gears of different sizes *Chain* *Drive wheel* *Pedal*

Watch gears

The back was removed from this wind-up watch so you can see the tiny gearwheels inside. Different-sized gearwheels are arranged so they will move the hands of the watch at different speeds. The clock is powered by a hand-wound spring. The spring turns a gearwheel that moves the minute hand. Another gearwheel slows down the movement that turns the hour hand.

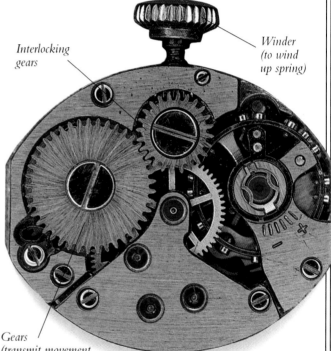

Interlocking gears *Winder (to wind up spring)*

Gears (transmit movement from the spring)

Belt drives

This picture of a factory, taken in about 1905, shows wide belts stretched between the machines and wheels in the roof. They are belt drives. The wheels in the roof are turned by an engine, and the belts transmit this movement to drive the machines.

MAKING GEARS WORK

*You will need: compass,
thick cardboard, scissors,
thick wooden toothpicks, glue,
2 brass paper fasteners,
small cardboard box.*

BEFORE engineers started using metals, they made gearwheels from wood. One way to make gearwheel teeth was to attach short wooden poles to the edge of a thick wooden disk. The poles on different gearwheels interlocked to transmit movement. Wooden gears were being used two thousand years ago. If you visit an old mill, you might still see similar gears today. The project on this page shows how to make a simple gearwheel system. After you have made it, watch closely how the wheels turn. They will turn in different directions, and the smaller wheel, with fewer teeth, will turn one and a half times for every one rotation of the larger wheel. The project on the opposite page shows how to make a simple belt drive that can turn an axle at different speeds.

3 Use paper fasteners to attach one wheel to the top of a box and the other to the side so that the teeth interlock. Turn one wheel to turn the other.

Make a set of gearwheels

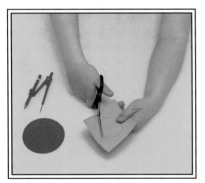

1 Use a compass to draw two circles on cardboard, with the diameter of one circle twice as big as the other; for example, 4 inches (10 cm) and 2 inches (5 cm). Cut out the circles.

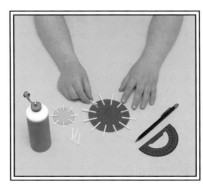

2 Glue four toothpicks around the edge of the small circle in a cross shape. Halfway between each two, glue four more. Glue 12 toothpicks to the large circle in a similar way.

Make a belt drive

1 Cut two holes in each long side of a box *(as shown)*. Slide a dowel that is 2 inches (5 cm) longer than the width of the box through each pair of opposite holes.

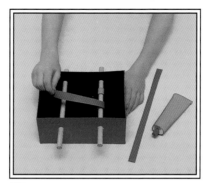

2 Glue a strip of cardboard to one of the axles. Wrap it around the axle and glue the end down to make a wheel. Make a bigger wheel on the same axle with a strip of cardboard three times longer than the first.

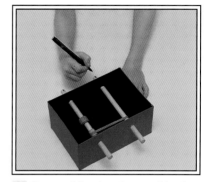

3 Put a rubber band around both axles. It should be slightly stretched when it is in place. Make a pen mark at the end of each axle so you can see how fast they turn.

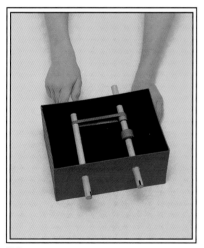

4 To test the belt drive, put the rubber band over the small wheel and start turning the plain axle. Does the wheel axle turn more or fewer times than the plain one?

MATERIALS

You will need: scissors, cardboard box, 2 dowels, strips of thin cardboard, glue, thick rubber band, felt-tip pen.

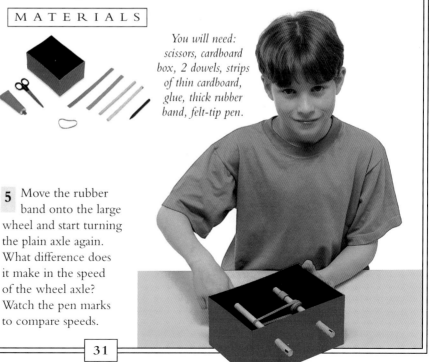

5 Move the rubber band onto the large wheel and start turning the plain axle again. What difference does it make in the speed of the wheel axle? Watch the pen marks to compare speeds.

POWER FOR MACHINES

Early machines, such as axes and ramps, needed human muscle power to make them work. Then people started using animals to work many simple machines. Animals can carry, pull, and lift much heavier loads than people can. Eventually, people realized they could capture the energy of wind and water to drive machines. Windmills and waterwheels were the first machines built to create power that could make other machines work. This power was in the form of movement energy, and it was used to do such things as grinding grain to make flour or pumping up water from underground. Today, the energy of wind and water is still captured, but it is used to create electricity, which we use to light and power our homes, schools, offices, and factories.

Windmills capture the energy of the wind. The whole building can be turned around so that the blades, which are also called vanes or sails, point into the wind.

Overshot waterwheel
There are two different types of waterwheels. One is called an overshot wheel *(above)*. Water flows along a channel above the wheel and falls into buckets on the wheel. The weight of the water turns the wheel.

Undershot waterwheel
A second type of waterwheel is called an undershot wheel *(above)*. Rushing water in a stream or river collects in buckets at the bottom of the wheel. The force of the water turns the wheel.

Grinding stones

Many windmills and waterwheels make power to turn millstones. The grinding stones in this picture *(above)* are used to squeeze oil from olives. Only the top millstone turns; the bottom one stays still.

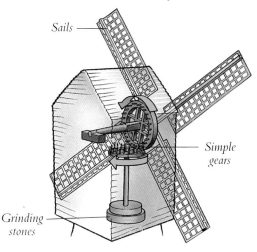

This drawing shows the inside of a windmill. The arrangement of wooden gearwheels transmits power from the sails to the grinding stones. Mills like this have been in use for centuries.

Sails

Simple gears

Grinding stones

Wind turbines

Wind turbines, like these *(below)* on a wind farm, are a modern type of windmill. The wind spins a huge propeller, which turns a generator inside the top of each turbine to produce electricity.

Hydroelectricity

A hydroelectric power plant makes electricity from flowing water. The water is stored behind a huge dam. As it flows out, it spins a turbine, which is like a very efficient waterwheel. The turbine turns a generator to make electricity.

WIND AND WATER POWER

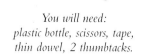

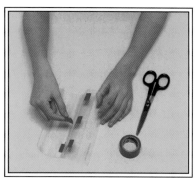

You will need:
plastic bottle, scissors, tape,
thin dowel, 2 thumbtacks.

MODERN windmills are called wind turbines. They are used to generate electricity. Hundreds of small wind turbines can be grouped together to make a wind farm. In some places, one or two large turbines generate enough electricity to power a small community. The most efficient wind turbines have only two or three blades, like the propeller of an aircraft. Wind turbines have several shapes; one is called the vertical-axis turbine because its axle is vertical to the ground. The project on this page shows how to make a vertical-axis turbine. It is one of the most efficient because it works no matter which way the wind is blowing. The project on the opposite page shows how to make an overshot waterwheel. This wheel can capture the energy of falling water to lift a small weight. Pour water onto the wheel from different heights to see if it makes any difference in the wheel's speed.

Make a windmill

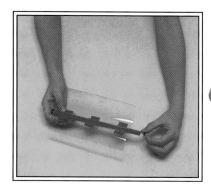

1 Cut off the top and bottom of a bottle and cut the middle tube in half to make two vanes. Tape the vanes together *(as shown)* with the edges overlapping 1 inch (2.5 cm).

2 Slide a dowel that is 1 1/2 inches (3.7 cm) longer than the vanes into the slot between the vanes. Press a thumbtack into each end of the dowel.

3 Hold the windmill at the ends only and blow on the vanes to make it spin.

Make a waterwheel

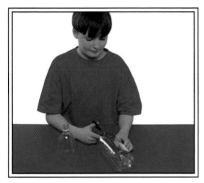

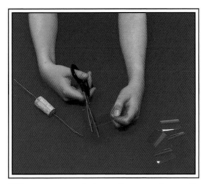

1 Cut off and save the top of a plastic bottle. Cut a small hole in the bottom near the base, so that water can drain out. Cut a V shape on two opposite sides of the rim.

2 Have an adult push wire through the center of a cork to form an axle. From the top part of the plastic bottle, cut six small curved vanes *(as shown)*.

3 Have an adult cut six slots around the side of the cork with a craft knife. Push the plastic vanes into these slots to form the waterwheel.

4 Rest the wire axle in the V-shaped slots on the rim of the bottle. Tape a piece of string onto one end of the axle and tie a small weight to the end of the string.

M A T E R I A L S

You will need:
large plastic bottle, scissors,
wire (have an adult cut
out the bottom of a wire coat
hanger), cork, craft knife,
tape, string, small weight,
large pitcher of water,
large plate.

5 With the waterwheel on a large plate or in the sink, pour water over the wheel so it hits the upward-curving vanes. The wheel will turn and lift the weight.

ENGINES AND MOTORS

Many modern machines get the power they need from engines and motors. Engines and motors are complicated machines themselves. An engine is a machine that makes energy for movement from heat. The heat is made by burning a fuel, such as gasoline. The first engines were powered by steam. Most engines today, such as the ones used in cars, are internal combustion engines, which means that the fuel is burned inside the engine. Gasoline burns inside a car engine, producing hot gases that push pistons up and down inside cylinders. The pistons turn a crankshaft, which carries movement energy from the engine to the wheels of the car. An electric motor is a machine that makes movement energy from electricity rather than from burning fuel. Most of the electricity we use is made in power plants or from the chemicals inside batteries.

A portable generator (above) has a small internal combustion engine, powered by diesel fuel, that turns an electricity generator. Generators are useful where there is no electricity or during a power outage, when the normal supply of electricity is interrupted.

Steam power

This locomotive is powered by steam. Steam was the main form of power in the 1800s. Steam engines are called external combustion engines, because the fuel burns outside the cylinders.

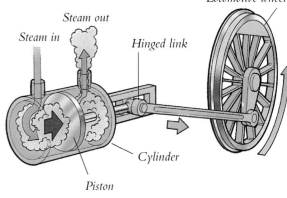

In a steam engine, steam made by heating water in a boiler is forced along a pipe into a cylinder. The pressure of the steam pushes a piston in the cylinder. The moving piston turns a wheel that drives a locomotive or powers a machine.

Engines for cars

A car has an internal combustion engine under its hood. In this picture, the engine's cylinders are inside the large black engine block.

Jet engines

Fast aircraft, such as military fighter planes, have jet engines. A jet engine creates hot gases that shoot out the back of the engine and push the aircraft forward.

Electric motors

An electric motor turns electricity into movement. When the motor is connected to a battery, its shaft spins around. Electric motors are small and clean, which makes them useful for household gadgets.

This electric motor has a colorful spinner on it. Two wires connect the motor to a battery, making an electric circuit.

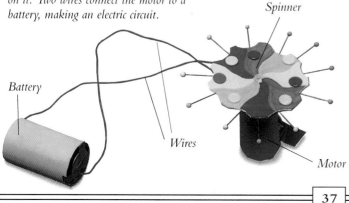

Spinner

Battery

Wires

Motor

HYDRAULICS AND PNEUMATICS

Not all machines are powered by engines or motors. Hydraulic machines are powered by a liquid, and pneumatic machines are powered by a gas. A simple hydraulic system is an oil-filled pipe with a piston at each end. Pushing one piston into the pipe forces the piston at the other end outward, transmitting power from one end of the pipe to the other. In a simple pneumatic system, compressed air forces a piston to move. Hydraulic and pneumatic machines can be very powerful. They are also quite simple and very sturdy. Machines that work in dirty and rough conditions, such as drills and dump trucks, often have hydraulic or pneumatic systems instead of motors. Most dental drills use a pneumatic system. Air is pumped to the drill making a tiny turbine inside the drill spin very fast. Air escaping from the drill makes a high-pitched whine.

This girl is lifting a book with pneumatic power. As she blows air into the balloon, the balloon inflates and pushes the book upward. Less effort is needed to lift the book this way than to lift it by hand.

Pumping air

All pneumatic machines need a device to draw in air from the outside and push it into the machine. This device is called an air pump, or compressor. A simple air pump *(below)* draws in air as the piston is pulled back and forces air out as the piston is pushed in.

Using an air pump is a simple way to blow up a balloon. A check valve in the pump's outlet lets air pass into the balloon as the piston is pushed in. The check valve also keeps the air from escaping when the piston is pulled back out.

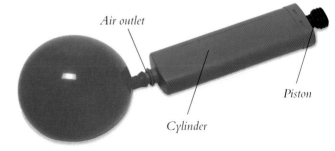

Air outlet

Piston

Cylinder

Hydraulic lift
Lifting a heavy load is easy with a hydraulic machine like this forklift truck. Hydraulic rams create the lifting force. Each ram consists of a cylinder and a piston. Pumping oil, or hydraulic fluid, into the cylinder makes the piston move in and out.

This simple hydraulic system has two pistons connected by a cylinder filled with hydraulic fluid. Using different-sized pistons creates a mechanical advantage. Pushing the small piston creates a greater force at the large piston.

The large piston is pushed out a short way but with greater force.

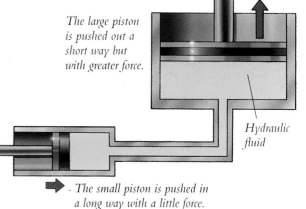

Hydraulic fluid

The small piston is pushed in a long way with a little force.

Check valve closed

Piston

Water in

Water out

Check valve open

Pumping water
Moving a water pump's piston in and out moves water from the pipe on the left to the pipe on the right. As the piston moves in, water pushes the check valve open and passes through. As the piston moves out, water presses the check valve closed.

Jackhammer
A jackhammer is a pneumatic drilling tool used to break through hard surfaces. The drill works like a hammer as its blade strikes the surface with great force. Here, you can see the hose leading from the air compressor to the drill.

LIQUID AND AIR AT WORK

You will need: large plastic bottle, scissors, airtight plastic bag, plastic tubing, tape, funnel, spray can lid, book (or another heavy object), pitcher of water.

HYDRAULIC machinery uses a liquid to transmit power; pneumatic machinery uses compressed air. The project on this page shows how to make a simple hydraulic machine that uses water pressure to lift a heavy object upward. Water is poured into a tube and fills up a plastic bag, forcing the bag to expand inside a narrow cylinder. The expanding bag pushes a platform upward, which, in turn, raises the heavy object. Many cranes, excavators, and trucks use hydraulic pressure to lift heavy loads. The project on the opposite page shows how to make a simple air pump. An air pump works by drawing air into one hole and pushing it out another. A check valve keeps the air from being drawn in and pushed out the wrong holes. When the air flows through the right way, the check valve opens, but, when the air tries to flow through the other way, it stays shut.

Make a hydraulic lifter

3 Place a spray can lid on top of the bag and rest a book, or another heavy object, on top of the bottle. Lift the funnel end of the tubing and slowly pour in water. What happens to the spray can lid and the book?

1 Cut off the top of a plastic bottle. Wrap the neck of an airtight plastic bag around the end of the plastic tubing. Tape the bag to the tubing to make an airtight seal.

2 Cut a hole near the base of the bottle. Push the bag and tubing through it so the bag sits in the bottom of the bottle. Tape a funnel to the other end of the tubing.

Make an air pump

1 Cut around a plastic bottle, about one third up from the bottom. Cut a slit down the side of the bottom part of the bottle, so it will slide inside the top part of the bottle.

2 Have an adult help you nail a wooden stick or dowel to the bottom of the bottle. The stick should be centered inside the bottle and nailed on from the outside.

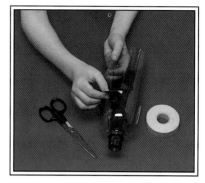

3 Cut a ¹/₂-inch (1.2-cm) hole near the neck of the bottle. Cut a 1-inch (2.5-cm) square of cardboard and tape one edge of it to the bottle to form a flap over the hole.

4 Drop a Ping-Pong ball into the top part of the bottle so it rests in the neck. Push the bottom part of the bottle (the piston) into the top part (the cylinder).

MATERIALS

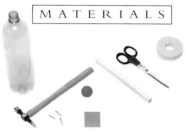

You will need: large plastic bottle, scissors, wooden stick or dowel, hammer, small nails, cardboard, tape, Ping-Pong ball.

5 Move the piston in and out inside the cylinder to draw in and push out air. Watch how the check valves work. The flap should close automatically when you pull out the piston.

MACHINES AT HOME

THE average home is full of machines. The kitchen, for example, has simple gadgets, such as can openers, faucets, scissors, and bottle openers, as well as complicated machines, such as a dishwasher. Other machines found in the home are washing machines, vacuum cleaners, and hair dryers. Even the zippers on your clothes are machines. Think about how each of these machines saves time and effort. What would life be like without them? Many machines not only save time and effort but also improve results. A modern washing machine gets clothes much cleaner than an old-fashioned washtub. Many household machines need electricity to work. Most of this electricity comes from a main supply system.

Zipper

A zipper is one of the simplest machines. Look carefully at a zipper fastener. It has a wedge in the middle that forces the two edges of the zipper together when it moves up and apart when it moves down.

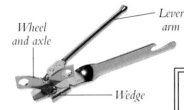

Wheel and axle

Lever arm

Wedge

Can opener
Can you see four different kinds of machines in a can opener? You should be able to find levers, a wedge, a wheel and axle, and a gearwheel. Together, they make opening a can easy.

FACT BOX

• The zipper was invented in 1893. The first zippers were unreliable until tiny bumps and hollows were added to the end of each tooth.

• Household machines powered by electricity were possible only after distribution systems for electricity were developed in the 1880s.

• One of the earliest vacuum cleaners was built in 1901. It was so large that it was pulled by a horse and powered by a gasoline engine.

• The idea of the spin dryer came from a French engineer in 1865, but it was not used until the 1920s.

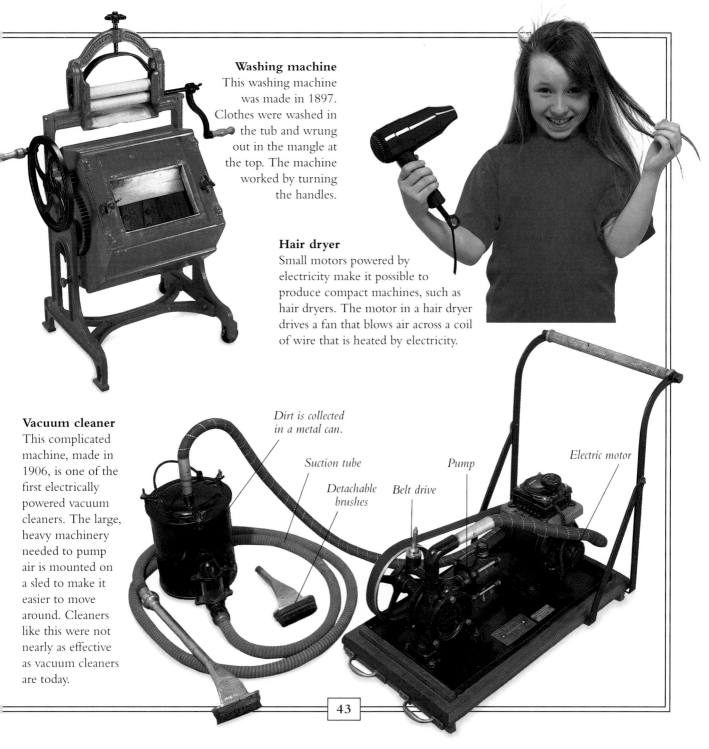

Washing machine
This washing machine was made in 1897. Clothes were washed in the tub and wrung out in the mangle at the top. The machine worked by turning the handles.

Hair dryer
Small motors powered by electricity make it possible to produce compact machines, such as hair dryers. The motor in a hair dryer drives a fan that blows air across a coil of wire that is heated by electricity.

Vacuum cleaner
This complicated machine, made in 1906, is one of the first electrically powered vacuum cleaners. The large, heavy machinery needed to pump air is mounted on a sled to make it easier to move around. Cleaners like this were not nearly as effective as vacuum cleaners are today.

Dirt is collected in a metal can.

Suction tube

Detachable brushes

Belt drive

Pump

Electric motor

MAKING HOUSEHOLD MACHINES

You will need: 2 planks of wood 20 inches (50 cm) long, 4 inches (10 cm) wide, ¹/₂ inch (1.2 cm) thick; hinge; screws; screwdriver; 2 plastic coffee-jar lids; glue.

SOME simple household machines are easy to make. The projects on these two pages show how to make a can crusher and a hand-operated vacuum cleaner. Use the can crusher to flatten empty soft drink cans before you recycle them. Crushing cans makes them easier to store and to carry. The can crusher uses a lever to press on the ends of the can. It is much easier to crush a can with a machine than with your hands. The vacuum cleaner uses the same principles to pick up scraps of paper as a regular vacuum cleaner does to pick up household dirt. Its design is based on the air pump made with the instructions on page 41. Use a heavy paper napkin for the collection bag because it allows air to pass through it as it filters out the bits of paper. Fastening the Ping-Pong ball to the neck of the air pump, instead of leaving it loose, helps the cleaner work better, because it keeps the ball from falling too far out of place.

Make a can crusher

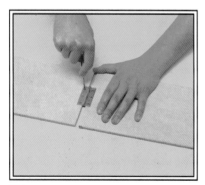

1 Lay two planks of wood end to end and have an adult help you join the planks together by screwing a hinge on the two ends that are facing each other.

2 Glue a coffee-jar lid (top side facing the wood) to each plank. Place the lid near the middle of the plank. Be sure each lid is the same distance away from the hinge.

3 To crush a can, put the can between the coffee-jar lids to hold it in place. Then, press on the top piece of wood.

MATERIALS

Make a vacuum cleaner

You will need: large plastic bottle, scissors, wooden stick or dowel, hammer, small nails, Ping-Pong ball, string, tape, heavy paper napkin, glue, tiny scraps of paper.

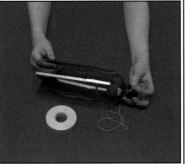

1 Make the air pump on page 41 but leave off the cardboard flap. Tape a piece of string to a Ping-Pong ball. Drop the ball into the top of the bottle and bring the string out through the neck. Tape the string to the neck so the ball can move only a fraction of an inch (cm) away from it.

2 Make a bag out of a heavy paper napkin. Glue it over the hole cut into the bottle. Air from the pump will pass through the napkin. The scraps will be trapped in the bag.

Modern vacuum cleaners have a powerful air pump driven by an electric motor. The pump draws air up through a tube and into a collection bag.

3 To pick up scraps of paper with the vacuum, quickly pull out the piston to draw the scraps into the bottle. Then, gently push the piston back in to pump the scraps into the paper napkin bag. How many scraps can you pick up with this vacuum cleaner? Can you think of any ways to improve it?

TRANSPORT MACHINES

Bicycles, cars, buses, trucks, trains, ships, and aircraft all are machines for transportation. They use many different types of engines, motors, gears, and wheels, and they all make it easier and quicker to travel from one place to another. A bicycle includes several types of simple machines and is designed to reduce effort to a minimum, but, of the transport machines that need human muscle power to work, it is one of the most complicated. Larger transport machines have engines and motors to power them. Many of them also have hydraulic, pneumatic, and electronic systems. These different systems combine to make the machine both efficient and safe.

The first bicycles did not have gears or pedals. They were called hobbyhorses. The rider had to push one along the ground with his or her feet, but they were still quicker than walking.

A bicycle's gear system lets the cyclist travel quickly or slowly while pedaling at a comfortable rate.

On your bicycle
A cyclist uses his or her own energy to push the pedals. The gear system needs this push to turn the rear wheel and drive the bike forward. Air hitting the cyclist's body, the weight of his or her body, and friction between the tires and the road all try to slow the cyclist down.

Tires and air
Tires are full of air to provide an easier, smoother ride. A pump is used to put air into a tire. A valve in the tire lets air in and keeps it from escaping.

Brake levers on the handlebars pull cables that press brake blocks against the wheel rims to slow the bike down.

Electric trains

The fastest trains, such as this French TGV, have powerful electric motors. The electricity to power them comes from overhead cables along the track.

Cars

All modern cars, from sports cars to family cars, have similar parts. They are powered by an internal combustion engine that burns gasoline or diesel fuel. The brakes use a hydraulic system.

Aircraft

Airliners, such as this Airbus A340, are very complex transport machines that can carry three hundred or more passengers at one time. They are driven by powerful jet engines and use hydraulic systems to control their flight. Safety is very important in air travel, so most of an airliner's systems have backup systems in case something goes wrong.

BUILDING MACHINES

CONSTRUCTING houses, office buildings, bridges, highways, and railroads involves digging into the ground; moving earth and rocks; and lifting and transporting steel, concrete, and other heavy building materials. Specialized construction machines, such as bulldozers, concrete mixers, and cranes do these jobs. Many of them use the principles of simple machines to work. For example, cranes use pulleys and balanced levers to help them lift. Most construction machines have large diesel engines to provide the power they need, and some have hydraulic or pneumatic systems to move their parts.

This sixteenth-century painting by Pieter Brueghel is called The Tower of Babel. *It shows people building with machines such as chisels, levers, pulleys — even cranes operated by huge treadmills.*

Earth mover
A bulldozer pushes away soil, rocks, and rubble to clear a building site so that work can start. Its wide tracks, called caterpillar tracks, keep it from sinking into muddy ground.

Digging out
A mechanical excavator digs up soil and rocks to make trenches for pipes and holes for building foundations. Its powerful digging arm is moved by hydraulic rams.

Moving mixer

A concrete mixer *(right)* carries concrete from the factory to a building site. Inside the drum, a blade that looks like a screw thread stirs the concrete. The blade stays still while the drum rotates.

Hammering in

A pile driver *(left)* pounds metal or wooden posts, called piles, into the ground. It repeatedly lifts a large weight with its crane and drops the weight onto the top of a pile. Piles form the foundation of a new building.

Towering crane

Tower cranes *(below)* might look flimsy, but they do not fall over, even when they are lifting heavy weights, because there is a concrete counterweight behind the cab.

FACT BOX

• A tower crane can build itself by increasing the height of its tower. The crane hauls up a new section, and ironworkers push it in place.

• Tunnels that go through soft rock, such as chalk, are dug with tunnel boring machines. The machine drills its way through the rock with a rotating cutting head.

• The cranes Romans used to build with, about two thousand years ago, were powered by slaves walking on a giant treadmill.

Dumping

Dump trucks deliver crushed stones, for building foundations, and take away unwanted soil. To empty a load, hydraulic rams tip the truck's box upward.

ON THE FARM

SOME of the oldest machines in the world are agricultural machines. Farmers use machines to prepare the soil, sow and harvest crops, and feed and milk animals. One of the first farm machines, and still one of the most important, was the plow. Archaeologists have found evidence of plows being used about nine thousand years ago. The first plows were simple, sharpened sticks used to turn up the soil. Today, a seven-furrow plow pulled by a modern tractor can cultivate 100 acres (40 hectares) of land in a day. Modern farming also uses specialized machines to make cultivated land more productive. In some parts of the world, powered machinery, usually operated by a tractor, does all the work. In many countries, however, plows are still pulled by animals, and crops are harvested by hand.

The spade is a simple machine for lifting and turning soil. A sharp blade makes it easy to push into the soil. The handle is a lever for lifting soil.

Steam power
The first type of tractor was a steam-driven traction engine. This one was built in 1880. It replaced the farm's horses and powered other machines, such as the thresher *(shown above)*.

Animal power
A water buffalo can pull a plow through the soil. Animals, especially oxen, are still widely used by farmers who cannot afford machines or who live in hilly areas.

Tractor and plow

Modern plows, pulled by tractors, are actually several individual plows in a row breaking up the soil into furrows. They make plowing a field much quicker than with a single plow.

Combine harvester

A combine harvester cuts and collects crops. A reel sweeps them into a cutter bar that slices off the stalks at ground level. Then, they are pushed into the machine where the grain is stripped from the stalks.

FACT BOX

• Combine harvesters often use screws, called impeller screws, or augers, to move grain around inside the harvester.

• The back end of a tractor has a rotating shaft, called a power take-off shaft. It powers machines that the tractor is pulling.

• One of the most important agricultural machines is the seed drill, which plants seeds in neat rows and at correct depths.

Milking barn

Machines can milk cows and pump the milk into containers for weighing and measuring. Then it is pumped into refrigerated tanks, collected by trucks, and transported.

PROJECT

MAKING FARM MACHINES

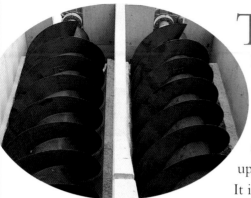

Inside an Archimedes' screw is a wide screw thread, or auger. Water gets trapped in this thread and is forced to move upward as the screw turns.

THE projects on these two pages show how to make two simple farm machines. The first one is an Archimedes' screw. In parts of the world where water pumps are expensive to buy and operate, Archimedes' screws are used to move water uphill for crop irrigation. This machine consists of a large screw inside a pipe. One end of the machine is placed in water and, as a handle is turned, the screw inside rotates, carrying water upward. This water-lifting machine has been used for centuries. It is named after the ancient Greek scientist Archimedes. The second machine to make is a simple plow. Pushing it through a tray of damp sand will show how the curved shape of a real plow lifts and turns the soil to make a furrow.

MATERIALS

You will need: small plastic bottle, scissors, plastic tubing, waterproof tape, 2 bowls.

Make an Archimedes' screw

1 Cut off the top and bottom of a plastic bottle and wrap plastic tubing around it to look like a screw thread. Attach the tubing with waterproof tape.

2 Put one end of the bottle in a bowl of water, resting it on the edge of the bowl. Turn the bottle slowly. As you turn, the water will pour out the top of the tubing. Catch it in another bowl.

Make a simple plow

1 To make the blade of the plow, cut a triangle of plastic from one side of a small plastic bottle.

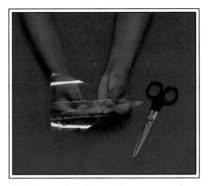

2 Cut a slot down the center of the triangle *(as shown)*. Fold the triangle in half along the line of the slot, against the curve of the plastic.

3 Use a thumbtack to attach the blade to the wooden stick. Make sure the blade is attached securely to the handle.

M A T E R I A L S

You will need:
small plastic bottle, scissors,
wooden stick or dowel,
thumbtack, tray of
damp sand.

4 Push the plow in a straight line through damp sand. Does it turn the soil and make a furrow?

This picture shows a wheeled plow from the 1400s. It has a wooden frame and an iron blade. The farmer guides the plow, while a helper keeps the oxen and horses pulling.

ELECTRONIC MACHINES

Most of the machines we use every day have moving parts that are operated by hand or by an engine or a motor. These machines are mechanical. Many modern machines, however, such as calculators and computers, have no moving parts. These machines are electronic. Inside an electronic machine, many different components connect to form circuits. The components control the flow of electricity around the circuits, which controls what the machine does. Complicated electronic circuits, with hundreds of thousands of components, can be contained on a single microchip only a fraction of an inch (centimeter) across. Some electronic machines, such as weighing scales and digital watches, have replaced the same mechanical machines. Many modern machines, such as robots, are combinations of mechanical and electronic parts.

An electronic calculator is a calculating machine with a microchip inside. Electronic signals in the microchip's circuit do the calculations.

Weighing scale

When an orange is placed on an electronic scale, it presses on a device called a strain gauge, which controls the strength of an electric current. Electronics inside the scale detect the size of the current and calculate and display the orange's weight.

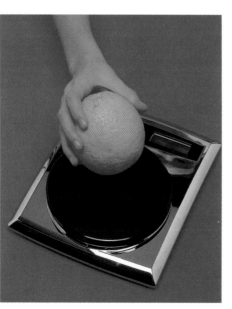

Computers

A computer is a multi-purpose electronic machine. The job it does depends on the program it is using. By changing programs, a computer can be used to play games, do complex calculations, paint pictures, or communicate with other computers.

The first computers

One of the first electronic computers *(right)*, called ENIAC (Electronic Numeral Integrator and Calculator), was built in the 1940s. It took up a huge amount of space because its electronic parts were thousands of times bigger than today's microchips. ENIAC needed several rooms for all its vacuum tubes, wires, and dials, yet it was less powerful than a modern pocket calculator.

Inside a computer system

A computer is an extremely complicated machine, but the way it works is quite easy to understand if you think of it in parts. Each part does its own job, such as storing or sending information.

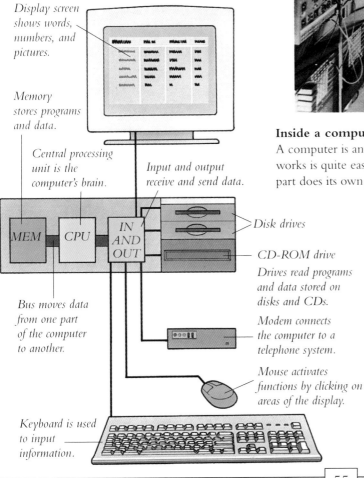

Display screen shows words, numbers, and pictures.

Memory stores programs and data.

Central processing unit is the computer's brain.

Input and output receive and send data.

Bus moves data from one part of the computer to another.

Keyboard is used to input information.

MEM CPU IN AND OUT

Disk drives

CD-ROM drive
Drives read programs and data stored on disks and CDs.

Modem connects the computer to a telephone system.

Mouse activates functions by clicking on areas of the display.

FACT BOX

• In the 1830s, British scientist Charles Babbage designed a mechanical calculator called an Analytical Engine. Unfortunately, it was never made because, although it would have worked, its parts were too complex.

• The first PC (personal computer) went on sale in 1975. It had 256 bytes of memory. An average PC today has 2 gigabytes of memory — more than 2 billion bytes.

• The fastest supercomputers can add together more than a million million numbers in one second.

MACHINES IN INDUSTRY

A circular saw has a razor-sharp blade with teeth that cut into the material as the blade spins. The material is moved backward or forward across the blade. This steam-powered saw is cutting logs.

MACHINE tools are used in factories to manufacture objects from metal, wood, or other materials. Machine tools cut, drill, grind, turn, and mill. Each of these tasks is done by a special machine. For example, a lathe is used for turning, and a saw is used for cutting. All machine tools have a cutting edge or blade, called the tool. The tool moves against the object being cut, called the workpiece. The tool shaves off unwanted material from the workpiece. Machine tools are used to make parts for engines and other machines with parts that must fit together perfectly. Industrial robots are versatile machines that can do many jobs, such as moving workpieces or drilling very accurately.

Turning

This pole lathe is powered by a foot-operated pedal. The lathe spins the workpiece around very fast. The operator presses cutting tools against the spinning wood, shaving away a layer each time. How accurately the workpiece is finished depends on the skill of the operator.

Pressing

This machine is called a die press. It presses flat sheets of steel into shaped panels, such as hoods for cars. The top part of the machine moves down to do the pressing. Each sheet of steel is molded to exactly the same shape every time.

Milling
This man is using a computer-controlled milling machine. A lathe spins the workpiece against a stationary wheel with teeth that cut away the unwanted material. A computer controls both the speed at which the lathe rotates and the position of the cutting tool. Computer-controlled machine tools make extremely accurate machine parts.

Cooling down
The milky liquid pouring over this cutting tool is oiled water. As the tool cuts into the metal workpiece, it gets very hot. The water keeps the tool cool, which stops it from melting, and washes away waste metal.

Industrial robots
Robots can weld car parts together. After the robot is shown how to do the job once, it can do it over and over again, much faster and more accurately than a human worker.

UNDER CONTROL

MACHINES that do complicated jobs need controls. Some of these machines need a human operator to control the machine manually. A car, for example, needs a driver to control its speed and direction. Other machines control themselves. Once they are turned on, they do their jobs automatically. An automatic washing machine, for example, will wash, rinse, and spin clothes with just a press of a button. One of the first machines to use a form of automatic control was the Jacquard loom. Punch cards fed into the loom told it which threads to use. Today, many machines are controlled by computers to perform set tasks as they are required. The most advanced machines are even able to check their own work and make changes, if necessary.

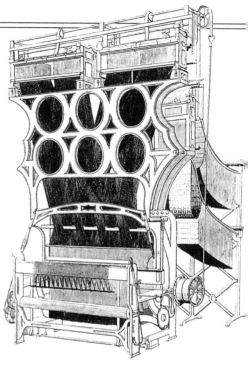

A Jacquard loom (above) from 1851 was controlled by punch cards. The holes in the cards set up the pattern that was woven into the cloth. Changing the positions of the holes changed the pattern.

Like clockwork
So they will keep the correct time, mechanical watches, like this one *(left)*, have a device called a regulator to control the speed at which their hands turn. The regulator ensures that the gears move at a regular speed.

Controlling speed
A steam locomotive's speed is controlled by a governor. When speed increases, the metal balls spin out to cut down the amount of steam going to the engine, which slows the engine down.

Governor

Industrial robots in car factories do many different jobs. These robots (right) are delivering parts to different areas of the factory. Lines on the floor guide them. Under the lines are wires that create a magnetic field. The robots detect this field and use it to follow a particular route. A central computer programs the robots to pick up and deliver parts around the factory.

Controlling traffic
Traffic signals are controlled by electronics. The next time you are waiting at a traffic light, look for the control box nearby. Some traffic lights can sense the approach of vehicles and are programmed to regulate the flow of traffic. Other traffic lights operate on a timer.

FACT BOX

• In the 1700s and 1800s, watchmakers demonstrated their skills by building moving figurines on clocks. These figurines, called automata, mimicked human actions, such as writing or playing musical instruments.

• Remote control means controlling a machine from a distance using either long wires or radio signals. Machines that work in dangerous conditions, such as at great depths under the sea, are often remote-controlled.

Many of the systems in this car of the future are controlled by a microprocessor, which continually receives signals from sensors and sends back control signals. It calculates the car's speed, distance, and fuel consumption and displays them on the dashboard.

AUTOMATIC CONTROL

Control a robot

ROBOTS are machines programmed to perform actions in ways similar to humans. Robots seem very clever, but they can do only what they are constructed to do. The project on this page will show how tricky it is to program a robot to do even simple jobs. Using only the words from the command list *(right)*, try to get a friend to successfully carry out the project tasks. The project on the opposite page shows how to make a simple control disk, which is the kind of device that controls some washing machines. The metal track on the disk is part of an electric circuit. As the disk turns, the track completes or breaks the circuit, turning parts of the machine, such as lights and motors, on and off.

MATERIALS

You will need: egg, blindfold, a friend, eggcup.

Robot commands
FORWARD
STOP
TURN LEFT
TURN RIGHT
ARM UP
ARM DOWN
CLOSE FINGERS
OPEN FINGERS

1 Hide an egg someplace nearby. Blindfold a friend and use the list of commands *(right)* to direct him or her to the egg.

2 Your friend should not know where the egg is or what to do with it. When the egg is found, instruct your friend to pick it up. Be sure to use only the commands listed.

3 Then, instruct your friend to put the egg down in another place. See if he or she can put it into an eggcup. How quickly did your friend complete these tasks?

Make a control disk

1 Using a compass, draw a 4-inch (10-cm) cardboard circle and cut it out. Cut a ring, about 1-inch (2.5 cm) wide, out of the bottom of the pie pan.

2 Glue the ring to the circle. Tape over the aluminum (as shown). The bare aluminum will complete the circuit. The tape will break it.

3 Mount the disk on a cardboard square with a paper fastener. Use metal wire to make two contacts with a bend in the middle (as shown).

MATERIALS

You will need: compass, ruler, cardboard, scissors, aluminum pie pan, glue, tape, brass paper fastener, metal wire, 3 plastic-coated wires, battery, flashlight bulb, bulb holder.

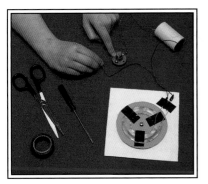

4 Tape the contacts to the cardboard so they touch the aluminum track. Use coated wires to link the contacts, a battery, and a flashlight bulb (as shown).

5 Turn the disk slowly. The light bulb should go on and off as the disk turns. When the contacts go over a piece of tape, the circuit is broken, and the light goes off. When the contacts touch the aluminum again, the circuit is completed, and the light goes back on. Do you know why the aluminum completes the electric circuit?

PERPETUAL MOTION

EVERY machine needs energy to make it work. The energy might come from a human or an animal, from fuel, from electricity, or from the movement of wind or water. When the source of energy is taken away, the machine will stop. Even if the machine is not doing any work, such as lifting or cutting, it will still stop because of friction between its moving parts. Friction is the force that acts like a brake on the movement of most objects. It occurs as objects move and rub against each other. Before inventors understood the force of friction, they thought it would be possible to build perpetual motion machines — machines that, once they were started, would keep on going forever.

You can feel friction at work by rubbing your hands together. The harder you press, the more difficult it is to move them. Can you feel the heat made by friction?

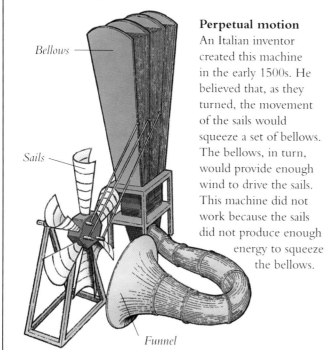

Perpetual motion
An Italian inventor created this machine in the early 1500s. He believed that, as they turned, the movement of the sails would squeeze a set of bellows. The bellows, in turn, would provide enough wind to drive the sails. This machine did not work because the sails did not produce enough energy to squeeze the bellows.

Bellows

Sails

Funnel

Flywheels
A grinding wheel, used to sharpen tools, is very heavy, but, instead of slowing it down, its weight creates a force, called momentum, that keeps it spinning. This kind of wheel is called a flywheel.

Overcoming friction

Moving things by rolling rather than sliding them reduces friction. These skates *(right)* have ball bearings around the wheel axles, where friction is the greatest. Bearings help the wheels turn smoothly, cutting down friction and wear. Bearings are used in the moving parts of machines, large and small.

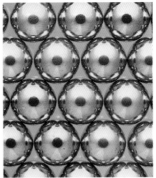

These ball bearings (left) *are suspended in oil. They are used to keep the moving parts of a machine separate so they do not rub together and cause friction. Bearings extend the life of the machine, because it is the bearings that wear out, instead of the machine.*

Frictionless space

An object moving through air and water also encounters friction. As it moves, the air and water resist the object and slow it down. Because there is no air in space, there is nothing to slow down a spacecraft after it has started moving. This might seem like perpetual motion, but it is not. Eventually, the spacecraft will crash into a star or a planet.

A racing car uses friction and tries to overcome it at the same time. Friction helps the car's tires grip the road. Its smooth, streamlined shape, however, is designed to reduce drag, helping the car travel faster. Drag is like friction. It slows down objects as they move through air.

GLOSSARY

adaptation – something used, often with adjustments or changes, in a way that best suits existing conditions.

ball bearings – metal balls on which some parts of a machine roll or slide to reduce friction.

belt drive – a system that moves machine parts by linking two wheels together with a belt or a chain (chain drive) that transmits the movement of one wheel to the other.

block and tackle – a rope and pulley system, used for lifting and hauling, in which the rope passes through one pulley anchored above (the block) and a second pulley suspended below it (the tackle).

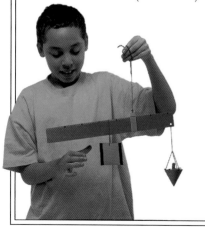

check valve – a valve that limits the flow of a liquid or a gas to only one direction at a time.

circuit – the path of electric current from the source of electrical energy to the end component and back to the source.

component – a main or important part of something larger that has many parts.

compressor – a machine that increases the pressure of air, or a gas, by squeezing, or pressing, it closer together in a smaller space than it normally takes up.

counterweight – a weight of equal size or force to balance a weight pulling in the opposite direction.

crane – a large machine, usually with a long, movable arm, that can both lift heavy weights and move them sideways.

crankshaft – a shaft or bar attached to the connecting rods in an engine that transmits turning energy from the engine to other parts of a

machine, such as the wheels on a vehicle.

cylinder – a tubelike chamber in a pump or an engine with fluid or gases inside that push pistons in and out to create movement energy.

device – a tool, machine, or piece of equipment made to be used in a specific way.

excavator – a large machine used for digging; a power-operated shovel.

force – strength or power, such as a push or a pull, applied to an object to cause movement.

friction – the force created when two things touch or rub against each other resisting movement between them.

gearwheel – a wheel with teeth around its edge that interlock with the teeth of another gearwheel to create movement.

gravity – the natural force that pulls all things toward the center of the earth.

hydraulic – moved by the

force or pressure of water or another liquid.

hydroelectricity – electric power that is produced by the force of flowing water.

inclined plane – a simple machine that consists of a flat surface, such as a plank or a ramp, set at an angle that is less than 90°.

lever – a simple machine that consists of a rigid bar that pivots on a supporting piece to pry up or lift a weight on one end by means of a pushing or pulling force on the other end.

mechanical advantage – the time saved and energy gained by using a machine to do work.

microprocessor – a computer processor (the part of a computer that processes data) contained on a microchip.

momentum – the force an object gains based on its weight and the speed of its movement.

perpetual motion – movement that, once started, goes on forever without interruption.

pile – a long column of wood, steel, or concrete driven into the ground to help support a large structure above ground.

piston – the sliding piece that fits snugly inside a cylinder. The pushing force of fluid, air, or gas in the cylinder moves the piston up and down or back and forth.

pivot – (n) the support on which a lever rests when it is lifting something; a fulcrum.

pneumatic – moved by the force or pressure of air or another gas.

punch card – a card punched with a pattern of holes that represents data. A computer reads the pattern and stores the data for electronic retrieval at a later time.

ratchet – a bar or wheel with teeth and a locking mechanism that allows movement in only one direction.

torque – a twisting force that causes turning or a rotating movement.

traction – pulling a vehicle by motor power; the grip something has on the surface over which it is moving.

turbine – an engine made of curved blades, or vanes, attached to a central drive shaft that is turned by the pushing force of steam, air, or water pressing against the blades.

valve – a device with a flap, plug, or some other movable part to start, stop, or control the direction of the flow of liquid or gas passing from one enclosed area to another.

vanes – thin, flat or curved blades attached to the top of a central shaft and turned by the force of water or air; the blades of a windmill or a propeller.

vise – a tool with two jaws, that usually open and close with a screw, to hold an object steady while working with it.

washer – a flat ring, often made of metal or rubber, used with nuts and bolts to help them fit more tightly.

BOOKS

Alternative Energy (series). Graham Houghton and Graham Rickard (Gareth Stevens)

Everyday Things and How They Work. Peter Turvey (Watts)

Fantastic Cutaway Book of Giant Machines. Jon Kirkwood (Millbrook Press)

Forces and Structures. Exploring Science (series). Keith Bardon (Raintree Steck-Vaughn)

Machines. Understanding Science (series). Clive Gifford (EDC)

Machines and How They Work. David Burnie (DK Publishing, Inc.)

Machines and Inventions. Record Breakers (series). Peter Lafferty (Gareth Stevens)

Mechanics. Steve Parker (Marshall Cavendish)

Mechanics Fundamentals. Funtastic Science Activities for Kids (series). Robert W. Wood (Chelsea House)

Toy Box Science (series). Gears. Levers. Chris Ollerenshaw and Pat Triggs (Gareth Stevens)

What's Inside Everyday Things. What's Inside (series). Peter Lafferty (Peter Bedrick Books)

The Wheel and How It Changed the World. History and Invention (series). Ian Locke (Facts on File)

VIDEOS

Computers and Robotics. (Lucerne Media)

Machines. Science: Start Here! (series). (AGC Educational Media)

Simple Machines. (National Geographic Society)

What Do You Want to Be When You Grow Up? Heavy Equipment Operator. (Big Kids Productions)

Work, Energy, and the Simple Machine (series). (United Learning, Inc.)

WEB SITES

www.mos.org/sln/Leonardo/InventorsToolbox.html

fly.hiwaay.net/~palmer/motor.html

Some web sites stay current longer than others. For further web sites, use your search engines to locate the following topics: *electricity, engine, equipment, hydraulics, machine, mechanics, power, turbine,* and *windmill.*

INDEX

pianos 10
pile drivers 49
pistons 36–41, 45
pivots 6, 7, 8, 9, 10,
  11, 12
pliers 4, 7, 10
plows 5, 20, 50–53
pneumatics 38–41,
  46, 48
power 6, 28, 32–39,
  40, 46, 47, 48, 50, 56
propellers 33, 34, 47
pulleys 6, 24–27, 48
pumps 38, 39, 40, 41,
  43, 44, 45, 46, 52

ramps
  (*see* inclined planes)
ratchets 16, 17
remote controls 59
resistance 6, 10

robots 54, 56, 57,
  59, 60
ropes 24, 25, 26, 27

saws 56
scales 8, 9, 10, 12, 13,
  23, 54
scissors 4, 7, 42
screwdrivers 4, 15,
  21, 44
screws 4, 6, 15, 20–21,
  22, 44, 49, 51, 52
seesaws 8, 9
shadufs 5, 7
ships 16, 25, 37, 46–47
slopes 18–19, 21, 22–23
spacecraft 63
spades 50
spin dryers 42

threshers 50
tires 46, 63

tools 4, 20, 39, 56,
  57, 62
torque 15, 21
tractors 50, 51
traffic signals 59
transport machines
  46–47
treadmills 48, 49
trebuchets 9
trucks 4, 28, 38, 39,
  40, 46, 47, 49, 51
tunnel borers 49
turbines 33, 34, 38
tweezers 10, 12

vacuum cleaners 42,
  43, 44, 45
valves (*see* check valves)
vehicles 14, 19, 23, 59

washing machines 42,
  43, 58, 60

watches 29, 54, 58
waterwheels 5, 32, 33,
  34–35
wedges 6, 20–21,
  22, 42
weight 6, 7, 8, 9, 11,
  12, 16, 17, 22, 23, 26,
  32, 34, 35, 46, 49,
  54, 62
wheelbarrows 10
wheels 6, 10, 14–17,
  19, 24, 25, 26, 28–31,
  32, 33, 34, 35, 36,
  42, 46, 53, 57, 62, 63
windmills 32, 33, 34
workpieces 56, 57
wrenches 4, 14, 21

zippers 42

PICTURE CREDITS

b=bottom, t=top, c=center, l=left, r=right